St. Margaret Middle School Library
1716-A Churchville Road
Bel Air, Maryland 21015

IN THIS SERIES

THE COMPOSITE GUIDE

to **SOFTBALL**

BRUCE ADELSON

CHELSEA HOUSE PUBLISHERS

Philadelphia

Produced by Choptank Syndicate, Inc. and Chestnut Productions

Senior Editor: Norman L. Macht
Editor and Picture Researcher: Mary E. Hull
Design and Production: Lisa Hochstein
Cover Illustrator: Cliff Spohn

Project Editor: Jim McAvoy
Art Direction: Sara Davis
Cover Design: Keith Trego

© 2000 by Chelsea House Publishers,
a subsidiary of Haights Cross Communications.
Printed and bound in the United States of America.

First Printing

1 3 5 7 9 8 6 4 2

Library of Congress Cataloging-in-Publication Data

Adelson, Bruce.
    The composite guide to softball / by Bruce Adelson.
        p. cm.—(The composite guide)
    Includes bibliographical references (p.).
    Summary: Traces the history of softball, explains how the sport differs from baseball,
and highlights notable players and games.
    ISBN 0-7910-5867-0 (hc)
    1. Softball—Juvenile literature. [1. Softball.] I. Title. II. Series.
GV881.15. A34 2000
796.357'8—dc21

                                                    99-085979

CONTENTS

1   A GOLD MEDAL SPORT

Although invented in the United States in 1887, softball has spread to many other nations to become one of the most popular team sports in the world. More than 42 million people from 104 countries were playing softball at the end of the 20th century. Teams from different nations play each other in many international competitions, including the Olympic Games.

In the United States, high school and college teams play softball. Youth softball is available for boys and girls. There are also hundreds of recreational leagues and teams, often sponsored by a business: a sporting goods store, florist, car dealer, or any other type of company. Team names often reflect the companies sponsoring them.

Since softball was invented, there have been many amazing games and players in what many people believe is the most popular team sport played in the United States. It is estimated that more Americans play in organized softball leagues than in any other team sport. Slow-pitch softball, with lots of home runs and high scoring games, is the most popular type of softball for people to play. But fast-pitch softball, where pitchers can throw the ball more than 90 mph, is also an exciting game to watch and play, with plenty of pitchers' duels and low scoring games.

As proof of softball's worldwide popularity, this sport received the ultimate international

U.S. Olympic softball shortstop Dorothy "Dot" Richardson drops the bat and heads for first. Richardson, who hit a home run during her team's game against China at the 1996 Olympics, helped the U.S. women win the first Olympic softball gold medal ever awarded.

Members of the 1996 U.S. women's Olympic softball team pose for a portrait on the field.

recognition in 1996 when women's fast-pitch softball made its debut as an Olympic sport at the 1996 Games in Atlanta, Georgia. The first Olympic softball gold medal was won by the U.S. women's team. This team, considered perhaps the best in the world, had an exciting time capturing the gold. But this is only part of the team's success story in international competition.

Before the 1996 Olympics, the U.S. team played in several exhibition and qualifying contests to see which teams would be selected for the Games. The U.S. team won 118 of the 120 games it played. This was an incredible record and made the United States the favorite to win the gold medal.

Once the Olympics started, the U.S. team began well, beating Puerto Rico, 10–0, and the Netherlands, 9-0. But after these first two wins, competition faced by the United States increased. The team scored only five runs and lost once in the three games before the gold medal match.

Australia defeated the United States, 1–0, in an exciting game that went into extra innings. The game seemed to be over after a home run by Dani Tyler of the United States in the 10th inning, until the umpire said the homer did not count. The umpire decided that Tyler had failed to touch home plate, a mistake that proved costly when Joanne Brown of Australia won the game with a home run in the bottom of the 10th. The United States also had a tough time in its next game, beating China, 1–0. Suddenly, with the American players struggling, opponents started believing that maybe the U.S. team could be beaten. Then, the Chinese team defeated Australia for the right to play the United States for the gold.

The game was played in Columbus, Georgia, which is near Atlanta. It began well for the Americans. In the fourth inning, Laura Berg led off with a single. Then, shortstop Dorothy "Dot" Richardson came to bat. (Richardson had led off the first inning with a single. In the third inning, she threw out Zhang Chunfang in an exciting play at home plate, preventing the Chinese team from scoring a run.)

When Richardson came up to bat in the fourth inning against pitcher Liu Yaji, she was ready to make more exciting things happen. With Laura Berg on base and the fans cheering her on, Richardson hit a long, high, fly ball to deep right field. The ball stayed close to the foul line. No one was sure if the ball would be fair or foul. Suddenly, the ball landed in the seats. The umpires decided the ball was fair. The home run gave the United States a 2–0 lead. Fans were cheering, clapping, and stomping their feet so loudly for the U.S. women that the stadium actually seemed to shake back and forth.

But there was a problem. The Chinese did not agree that Richardson had hit a home run. The manager, coaches, and players complained to the umpires that the ball was foul, not a home run. The arguments went on so long that the game stopped for about 10 minutes while the Chinese tried to change the umpires' minds. Finally, they gave up, and the game started again. Later, television replays of Richardson's hit proved the umpires were right. It was a home run. But the inning was not over. American player Julie Smith reached base on a throwing error and later scored when Sheila Cornell hit a line drive to deep center field that bounced off the outfielder's glove. The United States led, 3–0.

With her team in the lead, pitcher Michele Granger concentrated on preventing the Chinese from scoring. By the sixth inning, Granger had struck out eight batters, given up only three hits, and not allowed a run. But in that inning, the Chinese started a comeback. With two outs, Granger gave up a double to Liu Xuqing, which put runners on second and third base. Granger was then replaced by relief pitcher Lisa Fernandez, who quickly got into trouble. She threw a high, hard fastball that

Michelle Granger pitched for the U.S. women's softball team during the first half of the U.S. women's game against China. The U.S. women beat China, 3–1, for the gold medal.

the catcher was not able to grab. The ball sailed past catcher Gillian Boxx, and a run was scored. The U.S. lead had been reduced to 3–1. Fernandez knew the Chinese had a runner on base and could cut the lead to only one run on another wild pitch or a hit or error. With much excitement in the air and the fans cheering for the U.S. team, Fernandez ended the inning with a strikeout, preventing China from scoring another run.

Neither team scored again. When the game ended, the fans in Columbus cheered enthusiastically as the players celebrated winning the first softball gold medal in Olympic history.

There were many heroines on the U.S. team. Richardson was one of the stars of the gold medal game. The 34-year-old surgeon was also the U.S. squad's oldest player. Fernandez struck out 31 batters in the Olympics, more than any other U.S. pitcher. Sheila Douty, who played first base, led the U.S. women with nine hits in the Olympics while batting .393, good enough for number two on the team.

The story of the U.S. success did not end in the 1996 Olympics. After the excitement of winning the gold medal, the team began preparations for playing more softball and being selected for the 2000 Olympic Games in Sydney, Australia.

In 1999 the U.S. participated in the Pan American Games, an important test before the Olympics. The games took place in Winnipeg, a city in the Canadian province of Manitoba. All eyes were on the U.S. women to see if they could continue to play championship softball. Fans did not have long to wait for this team to start winning. In the first game against Colombia, Danielle Henderson pitched a perfect game, winning 9–0. She did not allow any Colombian batters to reach base while striking out 16 batters.

After three games in the tournament, the U.S. team was 3–0 and had not allowed its opponents to score any runs. In the fourth match, Lisa Fernandez, one of the 1996 Olympic heroines, was the starting pitcher against Cuba, also a very strong team. But Fernandez was not intimidated. She did not allow any Cuban player to get a hit, pitching a 5–0 no-hitter. Fernandez struck out 15 players. Only one Cuban batter reached base, on a walk.

By now, it was obvious to everyone that the U.S. team was still the world's best. Danielle Henderson proved this on August 3, 1999, when she pitched her second perfect game of the Pan Am Games, beating the Bahamas, 12–0. Four days later, the United States won the gold medal, defeating Canada in an exciting 1–0 contest. The United States won the game when Dot Richardson scored in the bottom of the eighth. This win gave the Americans a 12–0 record in the tournament and 42 straight wins in Pan American competition. In the tournament, the United States gave up only one run and outscored all of its opponents by the incredible score of 82–1.

Winning their fourth straight Pan American gold medal, the U.S. women showed the world that they would fight hard to win more gold medals in the next Olympic Games. Softball, now a worldwide phenomenon, had come a long way since its beginning more than 100 years ago.

St. Margaret Middle School Library
716-A Churchville Road
Bel Air, Maryland 21015

2 SOFTBALL BEGINS

Not surprisingly, baseball and softball are closely related. The two sports are like close cousins. While baseball was thriving in 1887, its cousin was about to be born.

Thanksgiving Day 1887 was particularly cold and windy in Chicago. Inside the Farragut Boat Club along the shores of Lake Michigan, several men escaped the icy cold and waited to learn the score of the Harvard-Yale football game. These men were all graduates of either Harvard or Yale, and they were curious about how their old schools were doing in this big game between the two rivals.

At that time, there were no radios, computers, or televisions to check for news and sports scores. Instead, people would wait for information to be transmitted over a telegraph or telephone. These 20 or so young men waited in the club to receive the news of the game. As each report was announced, cheers or boos were heard inside the hall, depending upon which team scored or who was winning. As they waited for updated reports to arrive, they would argue about which team was better and what would happen next.

Finally, the game ended. The last telegram said: Yale, 17 and Harvard, 8. One Yale fan, happy about the game's result, saw a boxing glove lying on the floor, picked it up, and tossed the glove into the air at one of the Harvard fans

Boys play mush ball on the roof of the New York City Boys' Club. Invented in Chicago in the 19th century, mush ball, also called pillow ball, uses a large, squishy ball that is difficult to hit far, making it suitable for indoor play or playing in confined areas.

on the other side of the room. Seeing the glove coming toward him, he quickly grabbed a stick and tried to hit the glove while it was still in the air. Making contact, the Harvard fan roared with excitement as the glove rocketed back across the room and over the head of the Yale fan who had thrown it.

One of the men in the room that day was named George Hancock. Seeing this glove-ball game, he quickly got an idea. He suggested playing an indoor ball game. Although his friends thought Hancock meant an indoor version of baseball, he really had something else in mind.

He picked up the boxing glove and began reshaping it. Hancock used the glove's laces to make it look like a large ball. He then drew what looked like a diamond on the floor of the club's gym with a piece of chalk. The diamond seemed like the ones on baseball fields, only it was much smaller. Hancock found a broom and broke off the handle to use as a bat.

Two teams were quickly chosen, and the first indoor ball game began. No records exist to tell us who played on each team and what each player did in the game. But we do know the final score: 41–40.

Everyone had so much fun that Hancock invited his friends to gather together at the club on Saturday, two days after Thanksgiving, to play again. This time, he promised, he would bring rules, a ball, and a bat with him. His friends quickly agreed. On Saturday, Hancock returned to the Farragut Boat Club with a large ball, not the boxing glove, and a small bat with a rubber tip. He painted white lines on the gym's floor and

called his new game "Indoor Base Ball." (At that time, the word "baseball" was spelled using two words.)

During the winter of 1887–88, people all over Chicago began playing this new game. Many teams came to the Farragut Boat Club to play Hancock's new sport. By spring, indoor base ball moved outside, where it was played on a field smaller than a baseball field. Now the game had a new name: Indoor-Outdoor.

In 1889 Hancock published a set of rules about his new sport. They made plain that this game and baseball, although closely related, had many differences. The rules said the game could be played in any room, using a large size ball and a bat 2³/4 feet long and 1¹/4 inches in diameter. The rules also suggested that players playing inside wear pads on their

Invented by George Hancock in 1887 as an indoor game, softball, which wasn't officially called softball until 1926, quickly became a popular outdoor game as well.

knees to prevent them from getting hurt while sliding on hard floors. These rules were adopted by the Mid-Winter Indoor Base Ball League of Chicago, the first league with teams playing this new game.

While Hancock's game was being played by more and more people, it was restricted to men. This changed in 1895, when the first women's team was organized at Chicago's West Division High School. Soon, women began playing in increasing numbers. At the end of the 19th century, women were not encouraged to play team sports. Most men believed that women were not strong enough to play strenuous games where they had to run and jump.

But softball, like field hockey and basketball, changed people's attitudes. Eager to play sports the way men did, many women began playing the new sport of softball.

In 1897 the first indoor league outside the United States was formed in Toronto, Canada. Despite its success, people soon stopped playing the indoor version of Hancock's game. Another new sport, basketball, was pushing indoor base ball out of the gym and onto the outdoor diamond. While indoor base ball was gradually fading away, the outdoor version of Indoor-Outdoor was spreading across the country.

In 1895, outdoor base ball became very popular in Minneapolis, Minnesota, with the help of Louis Rober, a local fireman. Looking for a game to keep the firemen busy when they were not out fighting fires, Rober turned to Hancock's sport.

On a vacant lot next to his firehouse, Rober laid out a simple diamond, with bases and a pitcher's mound, which was about 35 feet from home plate. For equipment, he used a small medicine ball and a bat with a two-inch diameter. Rober's version of softball was a hit at his firehouse and others throughout Minneapolis. He soon organized a team called the "Kittens." By 1900 rules were published for Rober's game, which became known as Kitten League Ball. This name was shortened to Kitten Ball some years later. By 1925, the game's name was officially changed by the Minneapolis Park Board to "Diamond Ball."

As the game grew in popularity, each part of the country developed its own set of rules. Different types and sizes of balls were also used. They could be anywhere from 10 to 20 inches in circumference. One ball, 16 inches around, was so big and soft it was called a mush ball.

Mush Ball, Kitten Ball, Diamond Ball, Indoor Base Ball, and Indoor-Outdoor were just some of the names given to softball in the sport's earliest years. The name "softball" did not appear until 1926, when it was suggested by Walter Hakanson, an official of the Young Men's Christian Association (YMCA) in Denver, Colorado.

Softball was now on its way to becoming a truly national game. The first steps toward achieving this goal were taken in Chicago, where the game was first invented. In 1933 Leo Fischer, a sportswriter for a newspaper called the *Chicago American*, and Michael J. Pauley, a businessman, organized a national softball tournament to be held at the Chicago World's Fair. Fifty-five teams went to Chicago to play softball. They were divided into three

The first national softball tournament was held at the Chicago World's Fair in 1933, and more than 350,000 spectators turned out to watch the three-day event.

groups: men's fast-pitch, men's slow-pitch, and women's.

The tournament was a big success and showed how popular softball had become. With free admission, about 70,000 people came to the World's Fair on the first day to watch the softball games. More than 350,000 people attended the three-day softball tournament. The first national softball champions were a women's team called the Great Northern Girls and a men's team known as the J. L. Friedman Boosters.

With the success of the tournament, word about softball spread to every corner of the country. A sport that was already popular became even more so. Hundreds of new leagues and teams developed. In 1934 the

Amateur Softball Association (ASA), founded in 1933 with the help of Leo Fischer, and other organizations produced the first uniform national softball rules. The ASA still exists today as softball's national governing body, promoting the sport across the country and supporting the U.S. men's and women's national softball teams that play in the Olympics and other international competitions.

3 SOFTBALL COMES OF AGE

Since its early days, softball has usually been played in the fast-pitch variety. This version of the game focuses more on pitching and defense than hitting. Low scoring games are common.

In softball's early days, pitchers dominated the fast-pitch game. They used different kinds of windups and motions to confuse batters. Many of these windups cannot be used today.

In 1909, Bart Holland, one of the new sport's earliest stars, pitched all 14 of the games his team played. Holland's team, Rock Island Railroad, played in the St. Louis Railroad Indoor League. Besides pitching all those games, Holland also pitched two no-hitters, struck out 247 batters, and gave up just 14 hits.

By the end of the 1930s, the fast-pitch game began changing. Rules were passed to make softball less of a pitcher's game and to give hitters more of a chance. In the mid-1930s, the pitcher's mound was only 37 feet and 8 inches from home plate. This short distance made it very hard for batters to hit a fast-pitch softball coming toward them at 90 mph or more. In 1936 the mound was moved back to 40 feet for men's games. By 1950, the pitcher's mound was moved 46 feet from the plate for men's games and 40 feet for women. These distances are still in effect today. In slow-pitch softball, the mound is 46 feet from the plate for both men's and women's games.

Emma Jean Lott, second baseman for the Lorelei Ladies, wings the ball to first base, while Jean Fitzgerald of the Tomboys slides into second during spring training prior to the 1955 major league softball season.

During World War II women softball players, including the Peoria Redwings team, above, formed the All-American Girls Professional Baseball League, which became the subject of the 1992 film A League of Their Own.

Other rule changes followed. In 1936 players were allowed to wear spikes for the first time. The next year, base runners were permitted to leave their base as soon as the pitcher threw the ball. Before this, base runners could not move until the pitch actually crossed home plate. In 1939 bunting was allowed for the first time in softball games.

While fast-pitch was changing, slow-pitch softball was becoming more popular. In slow-pitch softball, high scoring games with lots of home runs are very common, the opposite of fast-pitch softball.

When the United States entered World War II in 1941, softball followed the soldiers overseas.

By 1942, there were softball diamonds at just about every American military base in Europe, Africa, or Asia. After the battle of Guadalcanal in the Pacific, American soldiers built 20 softball fields there only a few days after the Japanese army had been defeated.

It was estimated that by 1943, more than one million U.S. soldiers were playing softball. Softball also continued to be popular for Americans at home. The best women softball players signed up to play with the All-American Girls Professional Baseball League (AAGPBL), which was founded in 1943 and operated until 1954. In 1992 this league was the subject of a movie, *A League of Their Own*.

The AAGPBL played a game that was a mix of softball and baseball. Players used a 10" ball, smaller than a standard 12" softball, but larger than a baseball, which had a 9" circumference. Pitchers in this fast-pitch league could throw the ball either underhand or overhand.

The AAGPBL players had to abide by the league's rules of conduct, which included wearing lipstick, dressing in feminine clothes when not playing baseball, and keeping a feminine hairstyle. Players were given etiquette lessons to ensure that they would be charming spokeswomen for their sport. As part of their spring training, the women of the AAGPBL went to charm school. The charm school guide encouraged the women to "be neat and presentable in your appearance and dress, be clean and wholesome in appearance, be polite and considerate in your daily conduct, avoid noisy, rough, and raucous talk and actions and be in all respects a truly All-American girl."

In 1946 and '47, Annabelle "Lefty" Lee Harmon was a pitcher and first baseman for the Peoria Redwings, one of the 10 teams that comprised the All-American Girls Professional Baseball League.

"They wanted us to act like ladies and play like men," said Annabelle "Lefty" Lee Harmon, who joined the AAGPBL at age 22 and played with the league for seven years. Harmon, who grew up playing fast-pitch softball, made a living playing a mixture of softball and baseball for the AAGPBL.

"Most of the ladies were between the ages of 17 and 30, so I guess the average age [for the All-American girls] was early twenties," Harmon recalled. "For the first two years of the league, 1943 to 1944, we had charm lessons. They taught us how to sit correctly, walk correctly, and put on makeup, and we walked up the stairs with books on our heads."

A dress code was also in effect for all of the league's players. "We traveled everywhere by chartered bus," said Harmon, "and we were not allowed to wear slacks or shorts in public. We had to change into our dresses before we got off the bus. But some of us wore long coats and pulled our pant legs up so it looked like we were wearing dresses."

One of the functions of the AAGPBL was to provide after-work entertainment for employees in the country's factories, which produced supplies for the military during World War II. When the war ended and gasoline was no longer rationed, people started traveling more frequently, and the popularity of the AAGPBL declined. "People were on the go after the war," explained Harmon. "Nobody was a homebody anymore."

The AAGPBL peaked in attendance in 1948, when 10 teams drew 910,000 fans, but attendance declined in later years. With the advent of television, men's major league baseball games were aired to national audiences, and the AAGPBL could not compete with this exposure. Faced with increasing financial losses and reduced interest, the league went out of business in 1954.

After the war ended in 1945, softball activity continued to grow. By 1953, slow-pitch softball had become so popular that the first Amateur Softball Association National Championship was held. Many recreational leagues and team from various businesses began playing this version of the sport.

By 1960, slow-pitch had surpassed fast-pitch in popularity. The all-men's American Professional Slo-Pitch League was formed in 1977, with teams in several large cities, such as Baltimore, Pittsburgh, Chicago, Detroit, and Cincinnati. Although about 2,000 people came to each league game, the league lasted only one year.

Today fast-pitch softball is played mainly by high school and college teams and in international competition. But there is also a professional league, where women are paid to play softball. Founded in 1997, the Women's Pro Softball League (WPSL) had teams in Virginia, Ohio, Georgia, Florida, and North Carolina. In 1999 the Tampa Bay, Florida, Fire-Stix won the WPSL Championship, defeating the Akron, Ohio, Racers.

Although Joan Joyce never had a chance to play in the WPSL or the Olympics, she is considered the greatest female fast-pitch pitcher

Joan Joyce, the greatest fast-pitch pitcher in women's softball, played 507 games during her career and lost only 33.

ever to play this sport. Born in Connecticut in 1940, she played mainly in the 1960s and retired from softball in 1975. In her long career, which included 17 seasons with the Brakettes of Stratford, Connecticut, she won 507 games and lost only 33. Joyce led the Brakettes to 14 national fast-pitch championships from 1966–1983. She also pitched 105 no-hitters and 33 perfect games. Joan Joyce could throw the ball very, very hard and fast. Her fastball was once estimated to travel at 110 mph. Joyce pitched 6,648 strikeouts in 3,972 innings. Besides pitching, Joyce was a first baseman and an excellent hitter. She finished her softball career with a .327 batting average.

In addition to softball, Joan Joyce was a three-time all-American in basketball and an excellent volleyball player and bowler. After retiring from softball, she became a professional golfer and toured the country, playing in many golf tournaments.

One of Joyce's most memorable achievements came in 1962. That year, she played in an exhibition where she pitched to Ted Williams, who had retired from playing major league baseball two years earlier. During his long career with the Boston Red Sox, Williams was considered by many to be the greatest hitter in baseball history. In the major leagues, he batted .344, the sixth highest career average ever, and he hit 521 home runs.

Joyce and Williams faced each other on a small field in Waterbury, Connecticut. About 18,000 fans crammed into the ball park to watch this historic matchup. Joyce threw 40 pitches to Williams in about 10 minutes. Of all these pitches, Williams was able to hit only two. He hit one foul ball and one single.

Joan Joyce and many others helped make softball the popular sport it is today. In 1990 a poll showed that about 16 percent of all Americans played softball. With millions of Americans playing this game, softball is the most popular team sport in the United States.

SOFTBALL AND BASEBALL

4

The rules, equipment, and structure of softball and baseball are very similar. This is not surprising, since softball was originally thought by some to be an indoor type of baseball. But there are some differences between the two sports. Here are some of them.

LENGTH OF GAMES

The length of a regular softball game is seven innings. A baseball game has nine innings. Both sports have extra innings if a game is tied after regulation play. Each game also has three outs per side.

DISTANCE BETWEEN BASES

The distance between the bases is one of the biggest differences between the two games. In fast-pitch softball, the bases are 60 feet apart. They are 65 feet apart in slow-pitch softball. In baseball, the bases are 90 feet apart. Slow-pitch games are often very high scoring because players do not have to run as far as in baseball to get a hit.

Softball pitchers pitch underhand, but the best fast-pitch softball pitchers can throw as hard as major league baseball pitchers.

BALLPARKS

Baseball stadiums can be quite large. In Yankee Stadium in New York, for example, the center field fence is 408 feet from home plate. Even in stadiums where professional baseball is not

*A softball player slides
into a base. The bases
are much closer together
in softball than they are
in baseball, and since
players do not have to
run as far to reach a
base, softball games
tend to be higher scoring
than baseball games.*

played, the fences can be far from home. In softball, the stadiums are not as big. Outfield fences are usually between 200 and 275 feet from home plate. This is another reason why there have been many great softball home run hitters, particularly in the slow-pitch version of the game. Softballs do not have to travel as far as baseballs do to be home runs.

BATS

Softball bats are usually made of aluminum. Aluminum bats were approved for softball play in 1969. They can also be made from bamboo, fiberglass, or another type of metal approved by the International Softball Federation. Softball bats cannot be more than 34" long

or thicker than 2 1/4". Softball bats can weigh no more than 38 ounces. They must also have rubber safety grips where the batter holds the bat. Major league baseball bats are made from wood. They can be 42" long and no thicker than 2". Baseball bats can also be heavier than 40 ounces. Athletes believe that it is easier to hit with aluminum bats than with ones made from wood since aluminum is a lighter material, making aluminum bats easier to swing than their wooden counter-parts.

BALLS

Softballs come in several different sizes. They measure 12", 14", or 16" in circumference. The standard softball is 12". Baseballs are much smaller. They have a circumference of nine inches. Which would be easier to hit, a large softball or small baseball? You might think the softball would be. But check out how close softball pitchers are to batters when they are pitching. You might change your mind, especially when you see how close fast-pitch softball pitchers and batters are, compared to their proximity in baseball.

PITCHING

Baseball pitchers are allowed to throw the ball either overhand or sidearm. Softball pitchers, either in slow or fast-pitch, can only throw the ball underhand. Pitchers also stand closer to the batter in softball than they do in baseball. In fast-pitch softball, the distance between

Softball bats are made from aluminum, making them lighter than wooden bats, and they are coated with rubber at the bottom to make them easier for the batter to grip.

pitcher and home plate is 46' for men and 40' for women, as mentioned earlier. But in baseball, pitcher and batter stand 60' 6" apart.

The two games are played similarly, with a batter hitting a pitched ball, running around the bases, and trying to score a run. There are nine players on the field in fast-pitch, just like baseball, but 10 in slow-pitch, with the 10th fielder usually playing in left-center field or behind second base in shallow center field.

Fast-pitch softball pitchers can throw as hard as major league baseball pitchers. But in slow-pitch, the pitcher lobs the ball to the plate. (A lob is a soft, underhand toss.) The best slowpitch pitchers throw the ball up in the air with an arc. The ball is coming down when it reaches the batter, who must time when the pitch has completed its arc so he or she can hit it solidly.

Baseball pitchers stand on a small hill in the center of the field called a mound. At the top of the mound is a white slab called the rubber. With one foot against the rubber, the pitcher throws the ball to home plate. But in softball there is no mound, just the rubber inside a circle in the middle of the field.

The name "softball" suggests that this sport is played with a soft, easy to handle ball. As anyone who has ever played the game knows, the ball is not soft at all. The earliest softballs were much softer than the ones used today. Early softballs probably had leather covers stitched around a handful of horsehair.

Horsehair softballs were eventually replaced by those made from kapok, a material found in trees in Asia and in various parts of the West Indies. Besides being used for

softballs, kapok has also been used to make mattresses, pillows, and life preservers. Kapok, unlike horsehair, is water resistant and moisture proof. Balls made from kapok did not get wet and heavy like horsehair balls did. Some softballs still contain kapok today.

Eventually cork replaced kapok at the center of softballs. The cork was molded into a round shape, wound with yarn, and covered with leather. Softballs with plastic centers were first used in 1970. Softballs have also been made with polyurethane centers covered by leather. Polyurethane, like plastic, is a compound that can be manufactured into many different shapes, weights, and strengths. Polyurethane softballs were first used in 1982.

Most softballs today have a combination of many of these materials. Their centers are made from cork wound with yarn that has been dipped in polyurethane to make it hard and then covered by leather. Balls can also contain a mixture of cork and rubber or kapok and polyurethane in the center. The centers of these balls are then covered by twisted yarn. Next, they are covered with leather made from cowhide or artificial leather-like material.

This sequence shows a softball pitcher's windup, release, and follow-through when pitching a fast-pitch softball game.

5

GREAT PLAYERS AND GREAT GAMES

While many sports fans know about great baseball players, little is known about softball's best athletes. Here are some of their stories.

In baseball, Mark McGwire holds the record for the most home runs in one season. He hit 70 in 1998. But in softball, 70 home runs in one year would not come close to the record. Softball's single season home run king is Mike Macenko, who played for Steele's Silver Bullets, a team sponsored by a softball sporting goods manufacturer in Ohio. In 1987 he hit an incredible 844 home runs. The next year, he hit 832 homers. In seven seasons, he clubbed 3,143 homers. This is more than four times the number of career home runs by Hank Aaron, major league baseball's all-time home run king with 755. Macenko's accomplishment is even greater when you consider that in all of baseball history, only 16 players have hit more than 500 home runs in their careers.

Besides being softball's all-time home run king, Mike Macenko holds another record. In 1995, 44 of the country's best softball players went to Detroit, Michigan. They participated in a hitting contest called "the Showdown in Motown." The contest took place at Tiger Stadium, where major league baseball's Detroit Tigers played until the year 2000.

"Mighty" Mike Macenko of Steele's Silver Bullets set a record in 1987 when he hit 844 home runs in a single season.

To win the competition, a player had to hit more home runs than anyone else. During the contest, Macenko did something no one in history had ever done before. He hit a softball completely out of Tiger Stadium. Amazingly, even though he made history with one tremendous home run, Mike Macenko did not win the home run contest—another player hit more homers than "softball's Mark McGwire."

In 25 seasons of playing softball, Mighty Mike Macenko hit an incredible 6,179 home runs. He once hit a softball 508 feet, the second farthest anyone has ever hit a softball. In 1988 he set a national softball record by hitting 10 home runs in one game and driving in 1,687 runs in one season. That same year, he belted 16 during a doubleheader in West Palm Beach, Florida.

Although he was a tremendous home run hitter, Macenko could do more than just hit for power. He also has a career batting average of .721. A 32-time all-American, Macenko won five national Most Valuable Player awards.

In addition to Macenko, Steele's Sports had three other power hitters who were known as "The Men of Steele"—Mike Bolen, "Crankin'" Craig Elliott, and "Mighty" Joe Young. Along with Mike Macenko, they hit 1,476 home runs and drove in 2,643 runs in 1986. Also that year the team won 217 games, lost 13, and won its second straight National Softball Championship. Steele's won a third championship in 1987, the year Macenko hit 844 homers.

Bruce Meade is another softball slugger. At 6' 7", weighing 275 pounds, he was a fearsome-looking hitter. Known as Mr. Softball, Bruce

Easily recognized by his powerful upper body and distinctive waxed mustache, Bruce Meade holds the world softball distance hitting record and is a member of the Slo-Pitch and National Softball Halls of Fame.

Meade was one of the game's most dominant players in the 1980s. He played on 17 World Championship softball teams and batted over .700.

Meade also holds the world softball distance hitting record: a 510-foot home run hit during a game in Amarillo, Texas, in 1978. Years later, in an interview with *The Softball News*, Meade described his record-setting homer:

> We're playing Port City Ford . . . And we were the defending national champions and these guys were thinking we couldn't beat them. Well, I came up and I knew their pitcher, Mike Pare, wasn't going to give me much to hit. But he would always give me one good one to hit. My adrenalin level was so high, and let me tell you, adrenalin goes a long way. Well, he gives me this

In 1944 "Bullet" Betty Grayson led her Portland, Oregon, team to the ASA's Women's Major Fast-pitch National Championship. One of the best softball pitchers of all time, Grayson encouraged young women to get involved in the sport and founded the Portland Softball School for Girls in 1952.

pitch on the inside corner [of home plate] and I just unloaded on it. The ball took off like a line drive. I mean, if the third baseman had been in the right place, he probably could've caught it. It really didn't start to climb until it was out of the park. . . . It was unbelievable. I mean, I'd never seen anything like it. When I got back in the dugout, I got a standing ovation. I had to come out and tip my hat. You just couldn't believe it unless you saw it.

Meade's tremendous blast was not measured until the next day. The fence his ball went over was 303 feet from home plate. The ball also carried over a second fence, 207 feet behind the first. Since they were measuring the home run the day after it was hit, no one knew for sure where the ball had landed. They just added how far both fences were from home, to get 510. Meade's homer may have traveled even farther than that.

Besides his record-setting homer in Amarillo, Meade is also known for being the only player to hit a softball for a home run in Houston's Astrodome. Meade's Astrodome home run landed 24 rows back in the outfield seats.

Although Bruce Meade established himself as a fearsome softball slugger, he was not always interested in the sport. In high school, he played many other sports but not softball or even baseball. Meade was a track-and-field star, excelling in the high jump and running. In college at East Tennessee State

University, where he majored in engineering, Meade continued his career as a discus and javelin thrower.

After college, he was not interested in playing softball at first. Only the slow-pitch version of this sport was available where he lived. There were no fast-pitch teams. But with the urging of some friends in the early 1970s, Meade began playing the sport.

At the height of his career, Bruce Meade worked hard to keep himself in top shape. He lifted weights five days a week and ran two miles a day, four times each week. Meade, also famous for being a Florida deputy sheriff and having a long handlebar mustache, is a member of the Slo-Pitch Softball Hall of Fame and the National Softball Hall of Fame. On display at the Slo-Pitch Hall of Fame is a container of wax he used to keep his mustache in shape.

There have also been many great women power hitters in softball. Laura Fillipp, who is also in the Slo-Pitch Softball Hall of Fame, was one of the sport's greatest female sluggers. In her career, she hit more than 200 homers and played in five Softball World Series Championships. Fillipp went on to coach college softball.

While there have been many great softball hitters, pitchers have also made their mark in the sport. In the 1940s and 1950s, fast-pitch softball was very popular. Three of the greatest fast-pitch softball pitchers of all time were Clarence "Buck" Miller, Harold "Shifty" Gears, and "Bullet" Betty Grayson—all members of the National Softball Hall of Fame in Oklahoma City, Oklahoma.

Elected to the Softball Hall of Fame in 1957, Harold "Shifty" Gears was the most dominating pitcher of the 1930s and struck out over 13,000 batters during his career.

One of the most dominating pitchers of the 1930s was Harold "Shifty" Gears. Some people believe that Gears got this nickname because he could pitch by using either hand, "shifting" from left to right. Others think he was nicknamed "Shifty" because of the tricky, "shifty" moves he used while playing basketball growing up in Rochester, New York. Either way, Harold "Shifty" Gears was probably the best pitcher of his time.

In 1934, Gears's first year with the Kodak Park team in Rochester, New York, he won 86 and lost only 4 games. In his career, "Shifty" Gears won 866 games, lost 115, threw 61 no-hitters, 9 perfect games, 373 shutouts, and struck out an amazing 13,244 batters. That's more than double the number of batters struck out by Nolan Ryan, baseball's all-time leader in this category. "Shifty" Gears even struck out Babe Ruth during an exhibition at Madison Square Garden in New York.

When he stopped playing softball, "Shifty" Gears taught children how to play the sport he loved. He was a softball coach for almost 30 years, from 1944 to 1973. Harold Gears was the first player elected to the National Softball Hall of Fame in 1957.

Inducted into the Softball Hall of Fame in 1960, Clarence "Buck" Miller had an outstanding softball career. Miller pitched 96 games in which no batter recorded a hit against him. To put Miller's accomplishment in context, consider that Nolan Ryan, who holds the baseball record for the greatest number of no-hitters, pitched only seven no-hitters throughout his career. In 1999, Ryan became a member of Baseball's Hall of Fame.

Betty Grayson threw the ball so hard she was called "Bullet Betty." In 1945 she pitched 115 straight scoreless innings. This is almost double the major league baseball record of 60 innings set in 1988 by pitcher Orel Hershiser. In her entire career, she won 456 games and lost only 99. Grayson also pitched 55 no-hitters and three perfect games.

Born in 1925 in Portland, Oregon, Betty began playing softball when she was 13 years old. Her first softball team manager thought she could be a great pitcher someday. Grayson, excited by her coach's confidence in her, told her dad what he had said. Seeing how much this meant to his daughter, he decided to help Betty achieve her pitching dream.

He and two pitchers helped teach Betty how to pitch. Her dad showed her the perfect pitching motion and windup for her to practice. And practice she did. Betty Evans (she added the name Grayson years later after she married) practiced everyday, no matter what the weather outside was like. Hot or cold, rain or shine, Betty Evans was outdoors working on her pitching, studying the suggestions her father and her other teachers made.

Eventually, Betty Grayson's hard work paid off. In 1943 she pitched for a Portland team in the first of her six National Championships. The next year, she led her team to

Softball Hall of Famer Clarence "Buck" Miller pitched an incredible 96 no-hitters during his career as a fast-pitch softball pitcher.

Hall of Fame pitcher Amy Shelton, shown in a 1957 photo, provided tough competition for Betty Grayson's team at the 1944 Women's Major Fast-pitch National Championship.

the ASA's Women's Major Fast-pitch National Championship. In the championship game, Grayson faced Amy Shelton, another great pitcher who would also be elected to the National Softball Hall of Fame years later. The game was an exciting one, with both great pitchers not allowing their opponents to score. Finally, in the 11th inning, Grayson's team was able to score the run they needed to win the game and become champions.

That year, 1944, was very special for Betty Grayson. Not only did her team win the National Championship, but she was named Oregon's Woman Athlete of the Year by the Oregon Sports Writers and Sportscasters Association. Grayson made even more of a name for herself in her hometown four years later when she played an exhibition game against several members of the Portland Beavers, a men's Class AAA professional baseball minor league team. She pitched to six Beavers, and only one got a hit against her.

Besides playing softball, Betty Grayson also enjoyed teaching girls and women to play the game she loved. In 1952 she founded the Portland Softball School for Girls. This school was so popular that the city of Portland eventually used it to teach softball to girls and women throughout the city. Betty Grayson retired from the sport in 1955. Inducted into the National Softball Hall of Fame in 1959, Grayson died in 1979.

Another great fast-pitch softball pitcher was Ty Stofflet from Pennsylvania. He could throw a softball as fast as 104 mph. In 1969 Stofflet was named an outstanding pitcher by the International Softball Congress (ISC).

In 1976, he pitched one of the most remarkable games in both softball and base-ball history. That year, Stofflet's team traveled to New Zealand to play a local team which had its own great pitcher, Kevin Herlihy, who would eventually be inducted into the Softball Hall of Fame. On February 4, 1976, the United States and New Zealand played each other in the town of Lower Hutt, New Zealand, for the International Softball Federation World Fast-pitch Softball Championship.

Everyone thought the game would be excit-ing. Stofflet and Herlihy were the star pitchers for their teams. They were also at the height of their careers. Once the game began, fans' expectations of a classic matchup were satis-fied. Stofflet and Herlihy engaged in a tremen-dous pitchers' duel. Inning after inning passed with the same results: United States, 0, New Zealand, 0.

As the game continued and no runs were scored, Stofflet and Herlihy both continued pitching. After 19 innings, both Stofflet and Herlihy were still pitching, and neither one had yet given up a run. There was no score.

Stofflet had retired the first 56 batters he faced. Every batter who came up to hit against Stofflet had turned around and sat back down in the dugout. The bases were completely empty of New Zealand base runners through 18 innings.

But this incredible streak could not last forever. In the 19th inning, with two outs, Stofflet hit Basil McLean with a pitch. After 18 2/3 innings, New Zealand finally had its first base runner of the game. But Stofflet did not let this mistake break his concentration or hurt his game. Staring at McLean standing at first base, Stofflet bore down, fired the ball toward home, and struck out New Zealand's next batter, ending the inning.

After 19 innings, fans were wondering which pitcher would tire first. In the top half of the 20th, the Americans finally broke through. Kevin Herlihy walked a batter. Another reached base on an error. Ty Stofflet then came up to bat. Hitting against his opposing pitcher, Stofflet concentrated hard on helping his team score. He singled, driving in Paul Troika with the game's first run. Stofflet's single was also his second hit of the game. It would be the last hit Herlihy gave up, but it was very costly. The Americans led the New Zealanders, 1–0. In the bottom half of the 20th inning, Stofflet retired the side in order, one-two-three, and won the game, 1–0.

Herlihy had pitched a brilliant game. He struck out 20 batters and gave up only five hits. But Stofflet was even better. During the 20-inning game, Ty Stofflet did not allow any hits or walks. He struck out 32 batters. Years later, Stofflet remembered this game as the highlight of his softball career.

Despite their brilliant pitching duel, Herlihy and Stofflet were unable to help their teams win the World Championship. Heavy rains and bad weather prevented the final championship games from being played. Unable to play, the United States, Canada, and New Zealand were declared tri-champions of the world.

Women's fast-pitch pitchers have also been known to throw hard. One of the greatest women pitchers in recent years was Kathy

Arendsen of Zeeland, Michigan. Known as "K.O. Kathy," Arendsen got her start in softball as a girl, going door-to-door to organize pick-up games in her neighborhood. She played softball in college and won the Broderick Award—reserved for the top collegiate softball player in the nation—three times.

In 1978, Arendsen signed with the Raybestos Brakettes of Stratford, Connecticut. In her 15 seasons with the Raybestos Brakettes, Arendsen pitched 79 no-hitters, 42 perfect games, and 265 shutouts.

Arendsen also has the distinction of being the first player to compete on the U.S., National, Olympic Festival, and World Championship softball teams. A four-time recipient of the Bertha Tickey Award for the outstanding pitcher in the ASA Women's Major Fast-pitch National Championship, Arendsen played on three World Championship-winning teams.

In 1981 she had a 36–2 record, striking out an average of 14 batters a game. In a celebrity softball game she struck out Yankees slugging star Reggie Jackson three times.

A 13-time ASA All-American, Kathy Arendsen played 15 seasons for the ASA's Raybestos Brakettes. In 1996, Arendsen, a college coach, became the youngest person ever elected to the ASA National Softball Hall of Fame.

After retiring from her playing career, Arendsen became a college softball coach. In 1996 she became the youngest person ever elected to the ASA National Softball Hall of Fame.

Great pitching also takes place in slow-pitch softball. Anrico David Pinto, a member of the Slo-Pitch Softball Hall of Fame since 1997, is one of the winningest pitchers in the game's history. In his career, this Myrtle Beach, South Carolina, pitcher won 610 games. By contrast, Cy Young's 511 career wins are the most in baseball history. Pinto, Slo-Pitch Softball Most Valuable Player in 1976, was also a big game pitcher. He won 16 Softball World Series games.

On September 18, 1993, Tim Schumacher pitched a no-hitter with a 16" softball. That was an amazing accomplishment because 16" softballs are very large and are usually easier to hit than smaller ones.

On June 8, 1991, Ann Maria Abbondanza played two softball games on the same day, one right after the other, while pitching for the Royal Construction Company team from Milford, Virginia. She won the first game, pitching a 2–0 no-hitter, and the second game, 24–0, pitching another no-hitter. On that day, she became the only woman in slow-pitch softball history to pitch back-to-back no-hitters on the same day. Only one baseball pitcher, Johnny Vander of the Cincinnati Reds, has ever thrown two straight no-hitters, but he didn't do it on the same day.

Softball has seen many great achievements since its development by George Hancock in the 19th century. The game that began as an indoor sport has spread outdoors and around the globe. With millions of participants world-wide and softball games taking place in over 100 countries, fans have many opportunities to see the best softball has to offer.

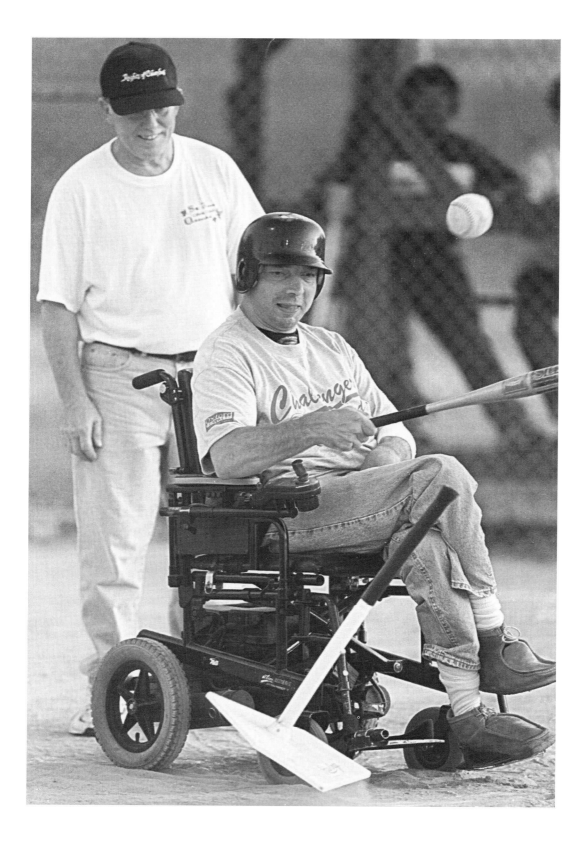

SOFTBALL IS
FOR EVERYONE

From its invention along Chicago's lake front on a cold, windy day in 1887, softball has become an international sensation. You can see this game almost anywhere—in schools, backyards, parks, or in international competition. Softball attracts more and more players each year—men, women, boys, and girls. It is played by people of all ages and backgrounds.

There is a league called Kings and Kubs in which no one under 75 can play. Since the 1950s, Kings and Kubs teams have played softball in many different locations across the United States.

From 15 million softball players in 1970, George Hancock's sport now attracts 42,152,250 participants each year worldwide. Of these players, approximately 60 percent are women. Many experts believe that softball is now played in more than 150 countries.

Although fast and slow-pitch are the most popular types, there are many other variations of this sport. Modified softball combines the best of both fast-pitch and slow-pitch.

In some places, softball is played on ice. In the winter of 1926 a softball game was played on skates in Cleveland, Ohio. There are also snow softball tournaments in Nebraska, Alaska, and Maine. In Idaho and Washington state, winter softball players wear snowshoes to play their games.

Ken Mask swings the bat as volunteer Joe Supple watches during the 1999 opening game of the Challenger Softball League in Oxford, Mississippi. The league provides individuals with mental and physical disabilities the opportunity to play softball at their own level.

Although the softball played in other countries is usually fast or slow-pitch, there are often small differences from country to country. For example, the Connaught Softball Association in Ireland requires each team to have at least six men and four women on the field and at least two substitutes ready to come into the game. Each team usually has between 15 and 18 members.

Mush ball, the game invented in Chicago in the 19th century, is still played today. Although this version of the sport has been played in Iowa and Wisconsin, it has never caught much attention outside Chicago, where it remains very popular. Basketball's Michael Jordan even played mush ball in a downtown charity game when he was with the Chicago Bulls. Mush ball is very much Chicago's game.

The mush ball is large, with a 16" circumference. It is also called pillow ball because at the end of a game, after the ball has been batted and thrown around the field dozens of times, it feels soft and squishy, just like a pillow. Many people give mush ball another name—cabbage ball—because the ball is large and round, like a head of cabbage. It is also called 16" softball.

According to the Chicago 16 Inch Softball Hall of Fame, "[16 inch softball is] the only sport every person that has grown up here has played at least once in school, a park district program, or at a picnic. No other city can make a claim like that."

Mush ball is a slow-pitch game. But unlike traditional slow-pitch softball, this is not a game where many home runs are hit. There are no Mike Macenkos or Bruce Meades in mush ball. Instead, players hit a lot of ground balls. The ability to play defense and catch the ball is most important.

Gloves are not used in this game, a tradition that goes back to the Great Depression of the 1930s. This was a difficult time for many Americans. People lost their jobs and had a hard time buying things, even food, for their families. With such financial difficulties, buying a glove for mush ball was considered a luxury. Although times have changed since the depression, mush ball players in Chicago have continued the gloveless tradition.

Another type of softball is called Over the Line or OTL. This game was invented on the

The Special Olympics, a nonprofit program of sports training and competition for individuals with mental challenges, prepares hundreds of athletes for softball competitions each year.

Softball is a game easily adapted to people with disabilities, as evidenced by these players, who are members of the National Wheelchair Softball Association.

beaches of California. Players do not use gloves or run the bases. There are two teams of three players each. When a batter comes up to hit, there is no pitcher to throw him the ball. Instead, a teammate kneels next to the batter and throws a softball up in the air for the batter to hit. There are only two kinds of hits in Over the Line—singles and home runs. All batted balls that fall behind the last fielder are home runs. The rest of the hits are singles. Over the Line has grown in popularity since its invention as a beach game. Today the game is played in more than 20 states.

Softball is also a popular sport for visually impaired athletes. Also called Beep Ball, the game is played with a 16" softball thrown underhand. Sighted players pitch and catch for their visually impaired teammates. When the pitcher is about to pitch, he shouts "Ready" so the batter knows the ball is on the way to home plate. The pitcher shouts "Ball" when the ball is close enough for the batter to hit. A machine inside the ball gives off a beeping sound to let the batter know when he should swing.

Once the batter hits the ball, he begins to run when he hears a buzzing sound from one of two four-foot pylons. These pylons, located along the third and first base lines, are like bases. When the batter hears the buzzing sound, he will run toward the pylon the sound is coming from. As he runs, the fielders try to locate the ball. Unable to see, they listen for the ball's beeping sound. If the batter reaches the buzzing pylon before one of the six fielders locates the ball, a run is scored. If the fielders find the ball first, the batter is out. Beep Ball is played throughout the United States. It has brought softball to those who otherwise would be unable to play America's most popular team sport.

Wheelchair softball is played mainly by adults. The National Wheelchair Softball Association is the game's governing body. The association sets rules, promotes the sport, and supports participating athletes across the country.

Players use a 16" softball. The rules of the game are basically the same as in Amateur Softball Association games, with only minor changes because the players use wheelchairs. Games are typically played on a cement or other hard-surfaced field. Each team must have one player who is quadriplegic—unable to use his arms and legs.

In 1999 two teams from St. Paul, Minnesota, battled for the 22nd National Wheelchair

A versatile game, softball can be played on foot or on wheels, as this rollerblading player demonstrates.

Softball Championship in Denver, Colorado. The teams, Rolling Thunder and the Saints, played an exciting championship game. The Saints led, 6–0, after three innings, but the Thunder came back in the fourth inning and scored four times, making the score 6–4. Then they tied the game in the sixth. Although the Saints went ahead, 7-6, in the seventh inning, many fans knew the game was far from over. The Saint Paul Rolling Thunder was the defending national champ, having won the title in 1998. In the bottom of the seventh, the Thunder's Scott Robeson doubled, driving in the tying run. With two men on base, Kevin Peterson won the game with a hard hit drive to left center field. The ball evaded the outfielders and rolled to the fence. Todd Anderson scored the go-ahead run, as the Thunder won, 8–7, for their seventh championship in the 1990s, making the St. Paul Rolling Thunder one of wheelchair softball's greatest teams.

Children who have physical disabilities can play adapted softball. This version of the sport is played on a basketball court or gym floor. Bases are placed closer to each other than in either standard softball or baseball. In adapted softball, the bases are 35 feet apart and the pitcher stands 20 feet from home plate. Since the game is played indoors, balls that hit off the walls are in play.

All of these versions of softball show how popular this sport is. Softball is certainly a game for everyone to play and enjoy, and from the looks of it, softball's popularity will continue to grow.

CHRONOLOGY

1887	George Hancock invents the game he calls indoor base ball in Chicago. The first game is played with a broomstick handle for a bat and a boxing glove for a ball.
1895	The first women's indoor base ball team is organized at Chicago's West Division High School.
1926	The word "softball" is first used to describe the sport Hancock invented.
1933	The first Softball World Championships for men and women are held at Chicago's World's Fair.
	The Amateur Softball Association is founded.
1934	The first national standardized rules for softball are established.
1936	One million Americans are playing softball.
1943	The All-American Girls Professional Baseball League is formed.
1953	Separate slow-pitch softball championships are held for the first time by the Amateur Softball Association.
1960	Slow-pitch softball becomes more popular than fast-pitch for the first time.
1968	The United States Slo-Pitch Softball Association is founded.
1970	15 million Americans are playing softball.
1990	In a Gallup poll, 16 percent of Americans say they play softball.
1996	For the first time in Olympic history, women's fast-pitch softball is a medal sport. The U.S. defeats China for the gold medal.
2000	More than 42 million people worldwide are playing softball.

GLOSSARY

All-American Girls Professional Baseball League – Established in 1943, this fast-pitch league featured the best women's softball players in the United States. They played a modified version of softball. Players used 10" balls, smaller than standard softballs, but bigger than baseballs. The league went out of business in 1954.

Amateur Softball Association – Also called the ASA, this is the national governing body for softball in the United States.

Indoor base ball – Invented in Chicago by George Hancock in 1887, this was the first type of softball. It was played inside, with a large ball and a rubber-tipped bat.

Indoor-Outdoor – In 1888, indoor base ball moved outside. Hancock's game was then played either in- or outdoors, which is how it received its name.

Kapok – This material is found in trees in Indonesia, the Philippines, Sri Lanka, Malaysia, and the West Indies. Kapok is water resistant and moisture proof. Besides being used in softballs, kapok has also been used to make mattresses, pillows, and life preservers.

Kitten Ball – Invented in Minneapolis by fireman Louis Rober in 1895, this softball game used a medicine ball and a bat with a two-inch diameter. It was called Kitten Ball beginning in 1900, after Rober's team, the Kittens.

Mush ball – This type of softball was invented in Chicago in the 19th century and is still played there. Mush ball is played with a 16" ball and no gloves.

Over the Line – Invented on California's beaches, this game has only three players on each side and no pitchers. There are only two types of hits—singles and home runs. Any ball hit over the last fielder is considered a home run.

Women's Professional Softball League – Formed in 1997, this league plays professional fast-pitch softball. In 1999 the Tampa FireStix won the WPSL Championship.

FURTHER READING

Atlanta 1996 Centennial Official Publication of the U.S. Olympic Committee. Salt Lake City, Utah: Commemorative Publications Inc., 1996.

Dobson, Margaret, J., and Becky L. Sisley. *Softball for Girls.* New York: The Ronald Press Co., 1971.

Hickok, Ralph, A. *Who's Who of Sports Champions.* New York: Houghton Mifflin Co., 1995.

Laing, Jane, editor. *Chronicle of the Olympics, 1896-1996.* New York: DK Publishing, 1996.

Markel, Robert, Marcella Smith, and Susan Waggoner, editors. *The Women's Sports Encyclopedia.* New York: Henry Holt & Co. Inc., 1997.

Nitz, Kristin. *Fundamental Softball.* Minneapolis, Minnesota: Lerner Publications Co., 1997.

Paluch, Mark, editor. *The Book of Rules.* New York: Facts on File Inc., 1998.

INDEX

PICTURE CREDITS Amateur Softball Association of America/National Softball Hall of Fame: pp. 2, 8, 27, 36, 39, 40, 42, 43, 44, 47, 54; Associated Press/WWP: pp. 22, 50, 58, 60; Corbis Bettmann: p. 11; Courtesy of Annabelle Lee Harmon and the All American Girls Professional Baseball League: pp. 24, 26; Courtesy of Doreen Hand, Special Olympics, New York: p. 53; Jeffrey Eisenberg: pp. 30, 32, 35, 56; Terri Lynn Herbst: pp. 17, 33; Doug Hoke/USA Softball/National Softball Hall of Fame: p. 6; National Archives: p. 14; New York Public Library: p. 20.

BRUCE ADELSON has written several books for children, including *The Composite Guide to Field Hockey* (Chelsea House Publishers, 2000), and *Grand Slam Trivia*, *Slam Dunk Trivia*, *Hat Trick Trivia*, and *Touchdown Trivia* (Lerner Books, 1998). His books for adults include *The Minor League Baseball Book* (Macmillan, 1995) and *Brushing Back Jim Crow: The Integration of Minor League Baseball in the American South* (University Press of Virginia, 1999). Bruce has also been a commentator for National Public Radio's *Morning Edition* and CBS Radio's *Major League Baseball Game of the Week* and the contributing editor for *The Four Sports Stadium Guide* (Random House, 1994). Bruce has also written about sports and other topics for *The Washington Post*, *Atlanta Journal-Constitution*, *Baseball America*, *Sport Magazine*, *USA Today's Baseball Weekly*, *The Daily Record*, *Baseball Digest*, and *Maryland Magazine*.

A book and multimedia reviewer for *Children's Literature*, Bruce is also a former practicing trial lawyer with 10 years of litigation experience, and a former elementary school substitute teacher in Arlington, Virginia.